OM Publishing
CARLISLE, UK.

Joni

A life of challenge

Sue Shaw

ISBN 1-85078-103-6
Copyright ©1993 OM Publishing .
Design copyright © 1993 Three's Company.
First published in Great Britain 1994.

British Library Cataloguing in Publication
Data

Shaw, Sue
    Joni : Life of Challenge
    I. Title   II. Bellwood, Shirley
    362.43092

    ISBN 1–85078–103–6

OM Publishing is an imprint of STL Ltd,
PO Box 300, Carlisle,
Cumbria CA3 0QS, UK

Designed and created by
Three's Company,
12 Flitcroft Street,
London WC2H 8DJ

Author: Sue Shaw
Illustrations by Shirley Bellwood

Worldwide co-edition organised and
produced by
Angus Hudson Ltd,
Concorde House,
Grenville Place,
London NW7 3SA

Printed in Singapore.

Hollywood . . . film stars . . . swimming pools . . . life in the fast lane. The film crew prepared for the next take. A handsome young actor sat at the wheel of a sporty open-top car. In the passenger seat, his leading lady, a pretty blonde girl, smiled.

The director shouted, 'OK. Roll it!' Cameras began to whir.

'Hey, great morning for a ride!' began the young man.

'Where?' the girl asked.

'Just a ride. Anywhere. Howsabout Florida?' he joked.

'Cut!' cried the director. 'That's a print.'

Everyone was relieved. No more takes for that day. The crew began to pack away their gear. The lighting man switched off the powerful spotlights. People started to move around – except for the girl in the car. She stayed patiently, watching the busyness going on around her. A woman appeared pushing a wheelchair.

'Hi, Joni. Sorry to keep you waiting.'

'Hi, Jay. That's OK. It's fun watching the action.'

Jay lifted Joni out of the car into the wheelchair. She bent down to put Joni's feet on the foot rests.

Wheelchair star

'This is hard work,' said Jay as she pushed the wheelchair over the thick rubber cables.

The 'star' in the wheelchair wasn't still acting. She really was paralysed. From her shoulders down.

Why was a Hollywood film company making a film starring a girl in a wheelchair? Film stars are usually strong and full of energy. They drive fast cars and always look fit. Joni couldn't even comb her own hair or wave to the cameras.

But the film was all about the girl in the wheelchair, Joni. She was playing herself in a film about her own life, so that people all over the world could understand how God can bring good things out of pain and suffering.

A sporting family

Until Joni was seventeen she had never really suffered. Life had always been full of fun and happiness. She lived with her parents and three sisters in Baltimore, near Washington, in the eastern United States of America. The whole family enjoyed the outdoor life. They played tennis and went swimming together. They spent holidays and weekends away, camping and hiking.

Joni's father had built a log farmhouse they called the 'ranch', set in rolling countryside, twenty miles out of town. Joni spent hours there riding her own horse, Tumbleweed. Her father taught her to ride when she was two years old, and she had won all kinds of ribbons and awards riding Tumbleweed at shows and gymkhanas.

Joni loved lacrosse the most. She was captain of the girls' lacrosse team at high school, where she was very popular with both the girls and the boys.

Joni's mum and dad loved each other very much and worked hard at loving their children, Kathy, Jay, Linda and Joni. Joni, the youngest, often had to explain to people that her name was pronounced Johnny – because she had been named after her father, John. The family name, Eareckson, showed that her father's family originally came from Sweden.

As she grew up her parents taught Joni how much God loved her. They were really pleased when, at the age of fifteen, Joni told them that she understood for herself that Jesus, God's Son, loved her and forgave her sins.

Joni soon joined in all the youth activities at her church. She had a Christian boyfriend called Dick, and worked hard to become a student at a nearby college. But deep down inside Joni felt there was still something missing.

She prayed to God, 'Lord, I want you to work in my life for real. I don't know how – I don't even know, at this point, if you can. But I'm begging you – please do something in my life to turn it around!'

Accident
Shortly after this prayer, Joni had an accident that was to change her life for ever. It was late afternoon on 30 July 1967. Joni, her sister Kathy and Kathy's boyfriend had gone on a trip to Chesapeake Bay on the east coast. Although the water was cold and murky, Joni decided to dive in for a swim. But the water was very shallow at that spot. Seconds after diving, she felt her head strike something hard.

Dazed, Joni lay face down on the sandy bottom, unable to swim back up. Realising something was wrong, Kathy dragged Joni's limp body up to the fresh air, then back to the beach.

'I can't move. I can't move!' gasped Joni, as a crowd of anxious people gathered round her.

Within minutes an ambulance arrived. With its siren wailing, Joni was taken to hospital and placed on a bed in the emergency unit. The doctor, who introduced himself as Dr. Sherrill, pricked her legs and arms with a long pin.

'Can you feel this?' he asked.

'N–no. I can't feel that.'

'How about this?' he said as he pricked her shoulder.

'Yes. Yes, I feel that.'

Other doctors appeared. Joni could hear them talking about her, but she couldn't understand their long medical words. Joni watched as a nurse injected her arm. She didn't feel a thing, but began to get very sleepy.

Strapped in

For the next few days Joni drifted in and out of consciousness. When she slept she had vivid dreams and nightmares. When she was awake she realised that she was strapped in between two canvas-covered frames, like a sandwich. Her head was held firmly by two metal tongs. This was to stop her injuring herself any more by moving her neck or head. Every two hours a couple of nurses would flip over the bed, called a Stryker frame, so Joni was facing either the floor or the ceiling.

Other patients in the ward were also in Stryker frames. Joni could hear some of them struggling to breathe because their lungs had been damaged. Two of the patients died, and this terrified Joni.

What if I die too? Why am I paralysed ? Joni thought, *Why won't the doctors tell me what's wrong? I'm going to die and they're afraid to tell me!*

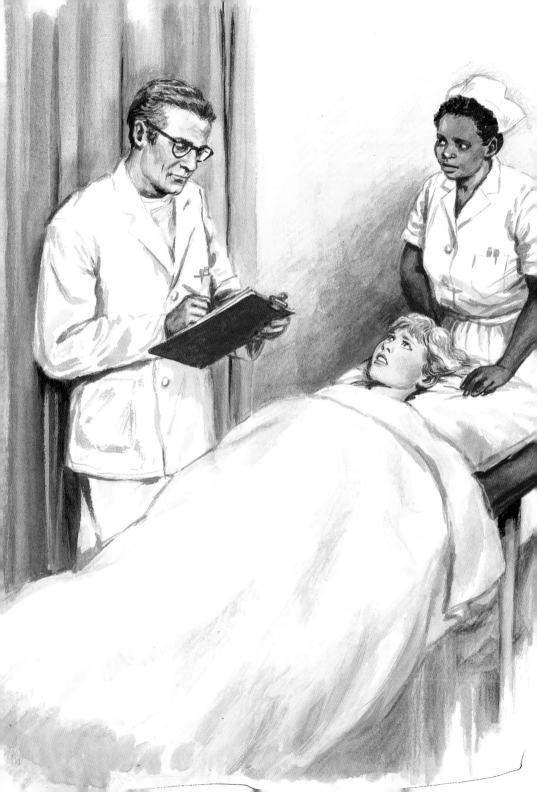

Friends and family visited every day. Her boyfriend, Dick, broke the hospital rules one day by sneaking a puppy into hospital inside his jacket. He held him close to Joni.

'Oh, he's beautiful,' said Joni as the puppy licked her face.

A nurse came in. 'How did you get him in here?' she asked.

'I came up the back stairs,' said Dick. 'You won't tell, will you?'

'Who, me?' the nurse said as she closed the door. 'I haven't seen anything.'

'What's wrong with me?'

Four weeks passed. As she grew stronger, Joni wanted to be told the truth.

'Dr. Sherrill, what's wrong with me?'

'You have a lesion of the spinal cord at the fourth and fifth levels.'

'I broke my neck?'

'Yes.'

'But that means I'll die.'

'Not necessarily. The fact that you've survived four weeks means you've passed the crisis.'

'So you thought I was going to die?'

'Many people don't survive accidents like yours. Now you've passed the crisis, I want you to use all your will power to get better.'

Joni felt excited and hopeful. She thought Dr. Sherrill meant she would be able to use her legs again. After an operation to join together the bones of her spine where they had been broken, Joni was moved into her own room.

'I know it'll take time,' she said to her parents and Dr. Sherrill, 'but I'll get better.'

'Will Joni be able to go to college next year?' asked her mum.

Dr. Sherrill's answer shocked them all.

'I'm afraid college will be out of the question.'

'You mean you don't know how soon Joni will walk again?'

'Walk? I'm afraid you don't understand, Mrs. Eareckson. Joni

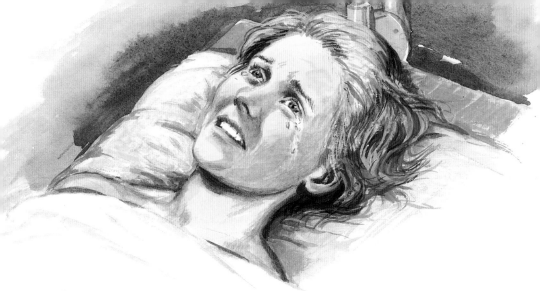

will never walk again. But we're hoping she'll be able to use her hands one day. Many people like Joni learn to drive, work and clean the house.'

'I want to die'

As soon as Joni was left alone she burst into tears. She knew her parents would be crying too. Life seemed so unfair. She had been active all her life. How could she spend the rest of her life paralysed? *God, I want to die*, Joni thought.

Lying in hospital day after day, Joni felt life was hopeless. The drugs she needed to take had made her lose her appetite and turned her teeth black. Her weight had dropped to just under six stone.

'Jackie, help me to die,' she said to a visiting high school friend one day. 'Give me something, pills, or cut my wrist. Please.'

'I can't, Joni. I can't!' Jackie sobbed.

'Help me end the suffering. I'm dying anyway.'

'Joni, I love you very much and it hurts me to see you suffer like this. But I can't do it.'

Joni begged Jackie several more times to help her to die. She felt so angry with God for letting her suffer like this. She was angry, too, that because of the paralysis she couldn't kill herself.

Dick came as often as he could and read aloud to her from the Bible. One day he read from the book of James. 'Listen to this, Joni. "Is your life full of difficulties and temptations? Then be happy, for when the way is rough, your patience has a chance to grow." Maybe God has let this happen to help your faith?'

Joni remembered how she had asked God to become more real in her life. Maybe this accident was going to help her?

She prayed, 'Lord, if I can't die, show me how to live.'

Training new muscles
Soon afterwards, the doctors said Joni should begin exercises to strengthen the muscles that she could still use. The physiotherapist explained, as she fastened Joni's arms into special slings, 'We'll have to train new muscles to do the work of the old ones. Try lifting your arms.' Joni tried. It felt impossible.

'Keep trying, don't give up,' encouraged the therapist.

After ten exhausting minutes Joni raised her arms about an inch. Day after day Joni worked in the slings. It was very painful and tiring, but little by little she began to raise her arms higher.

Soon she was strong enough to leave hospital and go to a centre called Greenoaks, where there was special apparatus to work on. She learnt to sit up again, and was allowed to sleep in an ordinary bed. She met lots of other people, some her own age, some younger, who were also paralyzed.

A high school friend, Diana, visited Joni every day. She always came with some new thought from the Bible to help Joni go on trusting in God.

A sad Christmas
By December, six months after her accident, Joni was allowed to go home for one day. She chose Christmas Day. Although it was good to be home again, Joni felt very sad as she remembered other Christmases.

Life will never be the same again, she thought. *I'll never be able to run out in the snow or go carol-singing.*

12

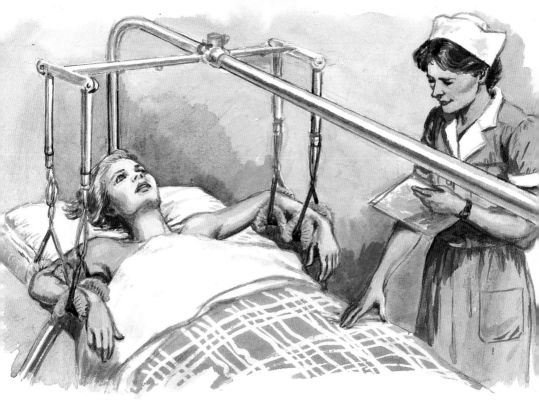

Back at Greenoaks she cried and cried. *What's the point of going on? All I do is sleep, eat and sleep. I can't face watching TV all day. If only I could do something.*

One day her therapist said to her, 'You could learn to write or type by holding a stick with your teeth.'

'No!' snapped Joni. 'That's disgusting. Why should I have to write with my mouth?'

'OK,' she replied, 'maybe another time.'

To her dismay Joni had to go back in the Stryker frame because her back and hip bone broke through her skin whenever she tried sitting up. The doctors decided to operate again, and chiselled away some of her hip and spine. But as soon as Joni bent her back the wounds burst open.

Back in the Stryker, Joni waited for the skin to heal over. Meanwhile another patient, Jim, talked to Joni about his ideas of God.

'I've done a lot of reading and studying,' said Jim. 'Life has no meaning. There can't be a God. Look at me. I'm crippled and what's God doing about it?'

Lying face down, with Jim's books open on the floor, Joni read his favourite authors. They were all people who doubted that there is a God who loves every single person in the world. Although confused, Joni still had some faith that God existed. She prayed, 'God, either you do exist or you don't. I want to believe, but I have nothing to hang on to. You've got to prove to me that you really do exist!'

Diana's surprise

Shortly after this her friend, Diana, gave Joni some surprising news.

'I'm going to drop out of college for a term. I can't decide what to do with my life, so I've got a job here at Greenoaks so that I can take care of you.'

'But Diana, you can't leave college!' Joni protested.

'I've prayed about it a lot, Joni. I believe it's what God wants me to do. I've made up my mind.'

It was good to have Diana around. She helped Joni and the other patients too. For Joni, Diana was an answer to her prayer. God was showing her that he existed and loved her by sending Diana to Greenoaks.

Although Joni still felt unsure, she decided to read her Bible again. She talked to Diana, too.

'I don't know why God let this happen to me. Maybe I'll never know.'

'Then work on getting out of here,' said Diana.

'But I'm scared. What'll happen when I go home?'

'God knows, Joni. Trust him. Even if you did know why God let it happen, would it make you happy? Just trust him to work it out. You can start now.'

'What do you mean?' asked Joni.

'Well, you could try writing with your mouth.'

'But I want to use my hands,' Joni protested.

'But what if you aren't able to?' said Diana.

Joni hadn't thought of that. The very next day she asked her therapist to teach her to write by holding a pen in her mouth. After many hours of practice, Joni could write letters, and was enjoying it too.

A *talent to paint*

A second back operation was so successful that Joni was told she would eventually begin to use a wheelchair. She began to sketch and paint. Her teacher was very impressed.

'You've got real talent, Joni.'

'But that was when I had my hands.'

'Doesn't matter. Hands are only tools. The talent comes from your brain.'

Joni began to spend more and more time painting and drawing. She was amazed at how well she was doing. She began to think more about God, too. As she wondered, *Does God really understand how I feel?* a picture came into her mind of Jesus on the cross.

Jesus knew what it was like to be paralysed, she thought. *On the cross he couldn't move his arms or legs. He knows exactly how I feel!*

This discovery was a great help to Joni. She started to read more and more about Jesus, and he became very important to her.

Christmas 1968 was drawing closer. This time Joni could go home in a wheelchair and stay for several days. She was fitted with a special corset to stop her falling forwards. Christmas was much more fun this time.

Even more exciting was the news that she could go to a new hospital in California, called Rancho Los Amigos, where the most up-to-date treatments were being used. Joni wept for joy.

'Maybe I'll learn to use my hands,' she hoped. 'Then Dick and I can get married.'

For three months Joni worked hard at new exercises. Braces were fitted to her forearms, and she learnt how to use her shoulder and back muscles to get her arms to move. In this way Joni learnt to feed herself with a spoon bent at an angle and fixed to her arm brace. To her joy, she became strong enough to use a wheelchair at last, and was given an electric-powered one. For the first time in over a year and a half Joni could move by her own efforts!

Reckless driving!
Sometimes she had wheelchair races down the hospital
corridors with another patient called Rick. One day Joni sped
fast round a corner trying to overtake Rick, and crashed into a
nurse. She sent a tray full of bottles and medicine flying. As
punishment for her reckless driving Joni had to promise to
drive only in low gear!

When the doctors told her she could go home, there was one important question she needed to ask.

'Will I ever be able to use my hands?'

'No, Joni. You won't ever get your hands back.'

In tears, Joni wrote to Dick. 'I'll always be helpless. I can never be a wife. God must have something else in mind for us. Let's just stay as friends . . .'

When she returned home, Joni tried to shut out other people and God.

God has let me down, she thought. *He didn't let me use my hands.* She began to spend more and more time day-dreaming and thinking about her early life.

'Stop it, Joni! Stop staring into space!' Diana shouted at her one day.

'Leave me alone,' said Joni.

'You've got to live in the present, Joni. The past is dead.'

Finally Joni accepted that her anger with God was getting her nowhere. She realised that the way she was thinking about God and trying to escape the past was as bad as actually doing bad things. The Bible calls this sin, whether it's a thought or an action. Joni saw that she was hurting God and herself.

'I'm sorry, Lord,' she prayed. 'Help me to live in the present. Please show me that my life has meaning.'

A new friend

When Joni told Diana how she felt and what she had prayed, Diana thought it would be a good idea for Joni to get to know her Christian friend, Steve. As soon as Joni met him she wanted to see him again. He talked excitedly about all the good things God was doing in his life and in the lives of other people he knew.

Once a week Steve came round with some other Christian friends to study the Bible with Joni. Again God had answered her prayer to know more about the Bible, by sending Steve. With his help, she began to understand how important it was to know God's word and obey it.

Steve was also able to help Joni to see things from God's side. Joni now knew she had a choice to make. Was she going to despair, or was she going to look to God, who could use even her suffering for her own good? Joni began to understand that if she let God in, he could use her suffering and pain to strengthen her character and her faith.

Living in the present
To help her live in the present, Joni decided to give away her sports gear and to sell her horse. By doing this, Joni accepted, and admitted to herself and other people, that she would never be able to play games or ride a horse again. She became a student at a local college and took a course on speaking in public. Deep down inside she felt God really did have a future planned for her – and the day-dreams came to an end.

Joni began to take more of an interest in her appearance. Her sister, Jay, and friend, Diana, helped her to buy new clothes, to put on make-up and change her hair-style. Joni also asked her family and friends to pray for her to become more loving and less selfish.

Invitations arrived asking her to talk about her faith to teenagers. *It's a good thing I took the speaking course*, thought Joni. She also helped form a singing group that was asked to perform at churches, youth clubs and special events.

After Steve left for college she missed him very much. Many of her friends were now married, and it was easy to feel left out. Like most girls of her age, Joni wondered, *Will I ever be married? Can I ever be happy without a husband?*

Falling in love
In the summer of 1970 she met Don Bertolli. She was now twenty-one and Don was seven years older. He was an athletic, handsome man, full of energy and fun. Joni admired his good looks and strong Christian faith. They began to spend lots of time together, talking, driving to the beach or countryside, watching films and meeting friends. It wasn't long before Don told her, 'I'm falling in love with you.' They began to talk about marriage.

Joni was very excited and happy. They also talked about asking God to heal her so she could walk again. They prayed together, and asked other Christians to pray as well. But no healing came. Don found this harder to accept than Joni. He grew quieter and more serious. It came as a great shock to Joni when he said that he just wanted to be friends.

'I'm sorry. I should never have talked about marriage. I was wrong. God didn't work the way I thought he would.'

'How can you say this? You can't mean it!' cried Joni.

'It's over, Joni. I'm sorry. Good-bye,' Don said quietly and left.

Shattered dreams

All Joni's hopes and dreams for marriage were shattered. Although hurt and confused, instead of being angry with God, this time she asked him for help. She remembered hearing someone say that God always gives us something better when he takes something away.

'I know, Lord, that you understand all my hurt. Please help me to trust you even more,' she prayed.

For the first time in her life Joni started to spend long hours drawing and painting. She saw her art as a way to show her feelings about what God was doing in her life. When she finished each drawing she signed it PTL, short for 'Praise the Lord'. Her work was so good that a local businessman organised an exhibition in a smart restaurant nearby. Much to Joni's surprise, she sold over one thousand dollars' worth of work, and television reporters turned up to interview her.

This was the beginning of a whole new way of life. More invitations came for Joni to show her pictures at art exhibitions, and to talk at schools, colleges and churches about her art and her faith in God. She was even invited to the White House, where she left one of her drawings for the President's wife, Pat Nixon.

Joni PTL

Joni was asked to give more radio and TV interviews. When she appeared on the 'Today Show' in New York, between twenty and thirty million people heard her talk about God and saw her artwork. So many people wanted to buy her work that she set up a greetings card business called 'Joni PTL'.

Before long Joni was a well-known personality. She wrote a book about herself called Joni, which sold thousands of copies. Many people who were suffering in all kinds of ways wrote to tell Joni how much her book had helped them.

World Wide Pictures wanted to turn her book into a film, and asked Joni to play herself. Although she wasn't trained as an actress, she agreed. She knew people would find the message of the film more powerful if it came from the real Joni.

For six months Joni worked in Hollywood, the film capital of the world. She lived in nearby Los Angeles with her sister, Jay, and Judy Butler, an English girl who worked for the Billy Graham organisation, which owned World Wide Pictures.

Even though she had been warned it would be difficult, Joni found it very painful to act out her past. Ten years had passed since her accident, but as she played the different scenes, Joni began to have doubts about God and to hate her wheelchair.

She was tempted to fall in love with one of the film crew, even though she knew he wasn't a Christian. There was little time for reading her Bible or prayer. She began to lose interest in food.

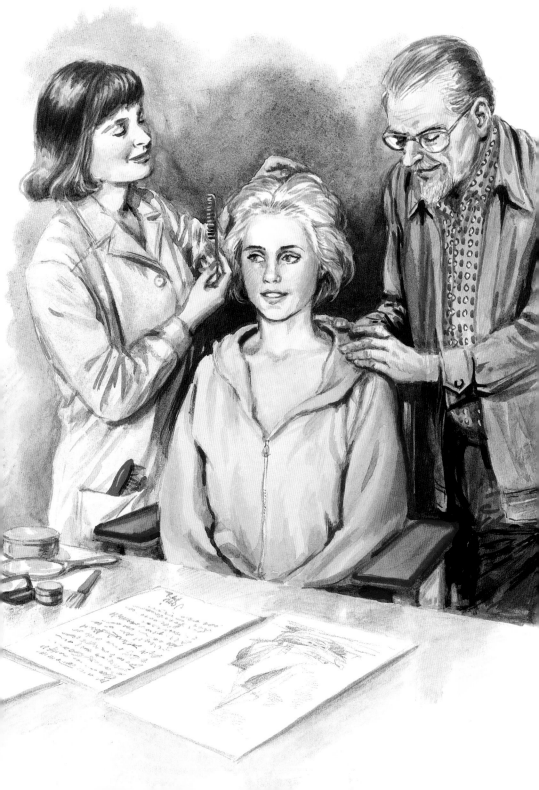

'I blew it!'
For the final scene in the film, the director wanted her to speak to 30,000 people at a Billy Graham meeting in Florida. At first Joni spoke with great confidence. Then she suddenly stopped. She had forgotten her lines. Tears filled her eyes. She started to say the first thing that came into her head. Even when everyone applauded at the end, Joni felt ashamed. *I blew it! I blew it in front of all those people*, she thought. She left Florida feeling a complete failure.

One day she visited Grace Community Church in Los Angeles and listened to the minister talking about the need to obey God in heart and mind, not just in what we do.

It's as if this is just for me! Joni thought. *God can see all the bad things that are going on inside me.*

Alone, Joni asked God for forgiveness. 'Lord, I'm sorry that I've been so full of wrong thoughts and feelings. I've been pretending to be close to you, but really I'm miles away. Please help me to serve you, and please don't give up on me.'

Back home in Baltimore, with a fresh determination to keep close to God, Joni started to make new plans for the future.

I'm thirty years old. It's time for change, to step out on my own, she thought. *There are thousands of handicapped people who don't have the kind of help that I do. It's time to try and do something.*

A new plan
The opportunity to make a change and help others came from Los Angeles, over three thousand miles away. Friends from the Billy Graham organisation invited her to work out a scheme to help handicapped people. It meant moving to Los Angeles, so friends from the Grace Community Church found a house near the church where Joni, her cousin, Kerbe, and old friend Judy Butler could stay.

It was difficult to say good-bye to her family and friends, but Joni, full of new hope, believed that God had something special for her. As the plane prepared to land, Joni could see the large white HOLLYWOOD sign jutting out of a hillside overlooking the famous city.

This is incredible, thought Joni.

One of the first people Joni met in Los Angeles was Dr. Sam Britten, who taught handicapped students at California State University. He gave Joni plenty of ideas for her scheme, but he also had an idea for helping Joni herself.

'I think you could learn to drive a van,' he said.

'But I don't have the muscles to turn a steering wheel,' she argued.

'No problem. You'll be on the highway in no time.'

He was right. Within weeks she was driving her own specially adapted van, a gift from Grace Community Church.

If my friends could see me now! she thought driving home. *I'm moving. I can go anywhere I want. Just like everyone else!*

Joni and Friends

This was just the start of many other exciting things that happened. With Joni's help, some of the other students at the university became Christians . Her dream of helping handicapped people became real. The organisation 'Joni and Friends' was set up to teach churches to use the talents of handicapped people, and to care for them.

In 1980 a new project called 'People Plus' began to train able-bodied people to help both mentally and physically handicapped people. Joni's days were filled with meetings, talks and caring for others.

One Sunday morning at church, because Joni found it hard to pay attention to the minister's talk, she began praying for a dark-haired Japanese man sitting in front of her.

'Please Lord, help this man to know you better. Give him strength. Keep him healthy. Help him to obey you,' she prayed.

Marriage

A few weeks later Joni spoke to the man she had prayed for. His name was Ken Tada and he was a history and games teacher, a weight-lifter, squash player, football coach and keen fisherman. They began to see each other a great deal. They were very happy together, and when Ken eventually asked Joni to marry him, she had no doubts.

On 3 July 1982, Joni and Ken were married at Grace Community Church. Now, as husband and wife, they both work very hard to make 'Joni and Friends' a success. They travel all over America and overseas, to tell those who suffer that God cares and can make something beautiful of their lives.